What Do You See?

A Book About the Seasons

by Sara Shapiro

Photo Credits:
Cover: (l) J.A. Kraulis/Masterfile, (tr) Bruce Burkhardt/Corbis, (cr) Tom Stewart/Corbis, (br) Richard Hutchings/Photo Edit;
p. 1: (fl) Farrell Grehan/Corbis, (l) Mark Tomalty/Masterfile, (r) dk & dennie cody/Masterfile, (fr) J.A. Kraulis/Masterfile;
p. 3: J.A. Kraulis/Masterfile; p. 4: Bruce Burkhardt/Corbis; p. 5: (tr) John and Barbara Gerlach/Visuals Unlimited,
(bl) Peter Griffith/Masterfile, (br) Masterfile/Masterfile; p. 6: (c) J.A. Kraulis/Masterfile, (br) Mark Tomalty/Masterfile;
p. 7: (tl) Tom Stewart/Corbis, (tr) Rommel/Masterfile, (bl) David Schmidt/Masterfile, (br) Masterfile/Masterfile;
p. 8: (c) J.A. Kraulis/Masterfile, (br) dk & dennie cody/Masterfile; p. 9: (tl) Strauss/Curtis/Masterfile,
(tr) Andrew Wenzel/Masterfile, (bl) J. David Andrews/Masterfile, (br) Boden/Ledingham/Masterfile;
p. 10: J.A. Kraulis/Masterfile; p. 11: (tl) Richard Hutchings/Photo Edit, (tr) Ron Watts/First Light,
(bl) Al Harvey/The Slide Farm, (br) Randy M. Ury/Corbis; p. 12: J.A. Kraulis/Masterfile

Copyright © 2009 by Scholastic Inc.

All rights reserved.
Published by Scholastic Inc.
Printed in the U.S.A.

ISBN-13: 978-0-545-16154-1
ISBN-10: 0-545-16154-1

SCHOLASTIC and associated logos and designs are trademarks
and/or registered trademarks of Scholastic Inc.

2 3 4 5 6 7 8 9 10   40   18 17 16 15 14 13 12 11 10 09

SCHOLASTIC INC.
New York • Toronto • London • Auckland • Sydney
Mexico City • New Delhi • Hong Kong • Buenos Aires

It is spring.
I can see buds on the trees.
These buds are green.

What do you see in spring?

It is summer.
I can see leaves on the trees.
These leaves are green, too.

What do you see in summer?

It is fall.
I can see leaves on the trees.
The leaves are red.

What do you see in fall?

It is winter.

I can see snow on the trees.

The snow is white.

What do you see in winter?

What season do you like best?

Spring

Summer

Fall

Winter

We like all
the seasons!